Seeing Is Believing

by Elizabeth Shub
pictures by Rachel Isadora

Greenwillow
Read-alone

GREENWILLOW BOOKS

A Division of William Morrow & Company, Inc., New York

"The Leprechaun's Trick" is adapted from an Irish folk tale,
"Pisky Mischief" from a Cornish folk tale.

Text copyright © 1979 by Elizabeth Shub
Illustrations copyright © 1979 by Rachel Isadora Maiorano

Design by Ava Weiss

Printed in the United States of America
First Edition
1 2 3 4 5 6 7 8 9 10

Library of Congress Cataloging in Publication Data
Shub, Elizabeth. Seeing is believing.
(Greenwillow read-alone books)
Summary: Two stories about Tom and the piskies,
"The Leprechaun's Trick" and "Pisky Mischief."
[1. Leprechauns—Fiction] I. Isadora, Rachel. II. Title.
PZ7.S5592We [E] 78-12378
ISBN 0-688-80211-7 ISBN 0-688-84211-9 lib. bdg.

For Ada, Ava, and Susan

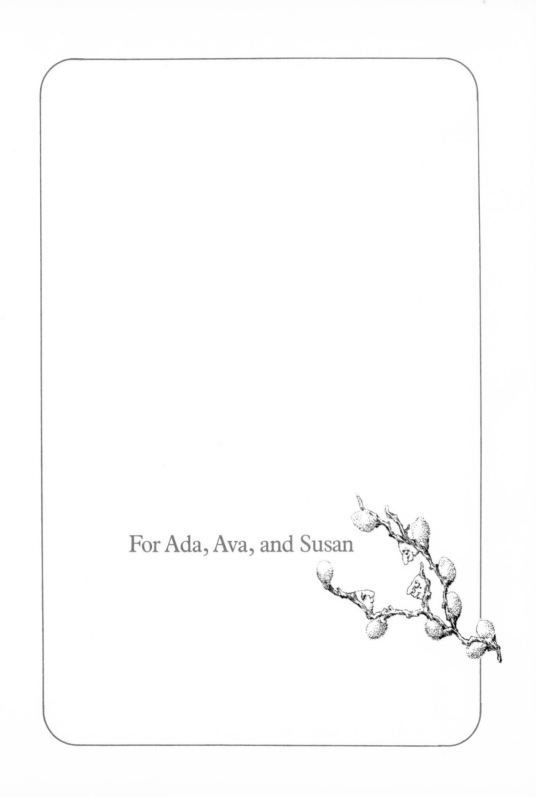

Contents

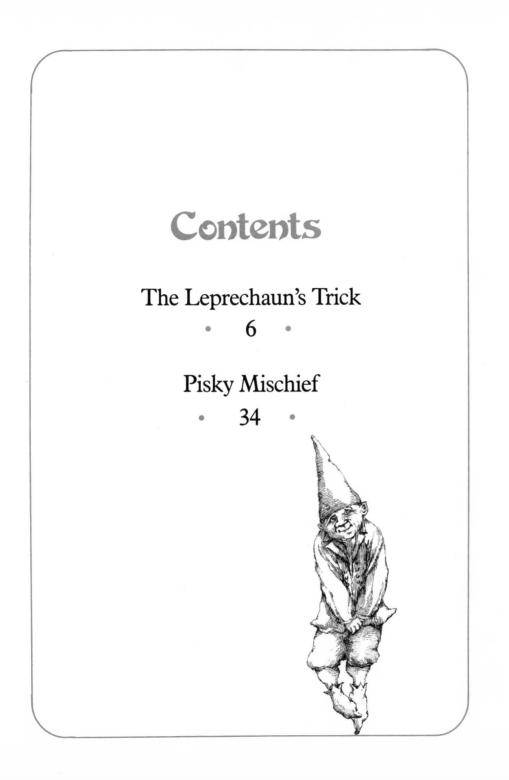

1·The Leprechaun's Trick

It was a holiday.
The sun was shining.
The air was crisp.
And it was long ago.

Tom was a farm boy
who lived in County Cork.
He said to himself,
"How lucky I am.
It is not raining
and I have no chores to do.

I will go for a walk."

Suddenly he heard an odd sound.
It came from behind a bush.
Tom peered over the bush.
There stood a tiny old man.
He was no bigger than a thumb.
He was dressed all in red,
except for a leather apron.
It was tied around his neck
and hung down to his knees.
On his head was a red peaked hat.
He was drinking noisily
from a jug
that he held in both hands.

When he had finished,
the little man sat down
on a tiny stool and
began to mend a shoe.
He was a leprechaun.
Tom knew it at once.

Everyone in County Cork
talked about elves and fairies.
But Tom had never seen one.
Nor had any of his friends.
"Seeing is believing,"
they said to one another.

And because
they had not seen any,
they were sure the little folk
did not exist.
And now here was Tom
face to face with a leprechaun.
What should he do?

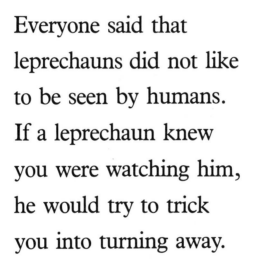

Everyone said that
leprechauns did not like
to be seen by humans.
If a leprechaun knew
you were watching him,
he would try to trick
you into turning away.

Once you turned, even for a second,
the leprechaun would disappear.
But as long as you kept him in sight,
he had to stay where he was.
Tom had also heard
that leprechauns always had
a treasure hidden away.
Tom thought, if I am clever,
I can find out where his gold is.
I will be rich and
I will buy a farm of my own.

Tom watched the leprechaun
hammering away.
Then he said in a quiet voice,
"How is your work going, neighbor?"

"Very well, thank you,"
  said the leprechaun.
"Why are you working
  on a holiday?" Tom asked.
"That is none of your business,"
  the leprechaun replied.
"What is in that jug?" Tom said.

"Magic brew,"
  said the leprechaun.
"What is it made of?" asked Tom.
"Heather," the leprechaun replied.
"Is it sweet?" Tom asked.
"That is none of your business,"
  the leprechaun said again.

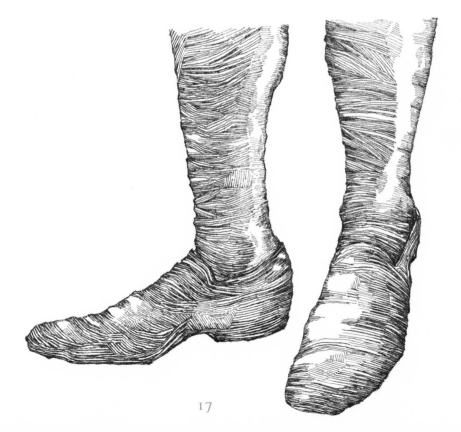

Now Tom wanted
more than anything
to taste the magic brew.
But the leprechaun
did not offer him any.
"Look at your cows," he said.
"They've broken into the oats.
Why don't you go after them?"
Tom was about
to turn his head,
but stopped just in time.
The leprechaun
had almost tricked him.

Tom was so angry,
he bent down and grabbed hold
of the little man.
In his haste
Tom knocked over the jug
and all the magic brew
spilled out.

Tom grew angrier still.
He held the leprechaun
in his fist and said,
"Don't try to trick me.
Just tell me where
your gold is."
The leprechaun
could not get away.

He motioned with his head.
"Take that path," he said,
"and I will show you
where my gold is buried."
Tom set off at once.
He did not take his eyes
off the leprechaun.

They crossed ditches and a bog.
They climbed over fences.
At last they came
to a field of ragweed.

The leprechaun pointed
to one of the weeds.
"Dig under that one," he said.
"And now you don't need me
anymore, do you?"

Tom laughed loudly.
"No, I don't," he said.
He put the leprechaun down.
"Good-bye," said the leprechaun.
"And may what you find
be your just reward."
The leprechaun jumped
behind a ragweed
and was gone.

Tom could not wait to dig.
But he had nothing to dig with.
He had to go home
and get a spade.
But how would he know
the right ragweed
when he returned?
"This will do nicely,"
he said to himself.
He took off
one of his red garters
and tied it on the ragweed.

Then Tom ran home
and came back with a spade.
But when he reached the field,
he did not know
which way to turn.

There were acres of ragweed.
And each and every plant
had a red garter tied on it.
Tom could not tell
which garter was his.
The leprechaun
had tricked him after all.

Tom walked sadly home.
And just out of sight,
behind him,
followed
the leprechaun.

He spun along,
upside down,

balanced on the tip
of his red peaked hat.

There was no mistaking
how pleased he was
with himself.

Tom never told anyone
about his meeting
with the leprechaun.
But the next time the talk
turned to the little folk
and Tom's friends said
they didn't believe
in elves or fairies,
Tom surprised everyone
by announcing firmly,
"Well, I do!"

2·Pisky Mischief

Tom never saw
the leprechaun again.
And he never found
the buried gold.
But as luck would have it,
he did get a farm
of his own.

Tom had an uncle
in Cornwall.
He was an old man,
and when he died,
he left his farm to Tom.

Tom moved to Cornwall,
and married a girl
named Griselda.
Tom and Griselda worked hard
and they were happy.

As the years went by,
Tom thought less and less
about the leprechaun
and his gold.

It was market day.
The sun was shining.
The air was crisp.
Tom said to himself,
"How lucky I am.
It is not raining
and I am going to market."
He saddled his mare, Bess.
He promised Griselda
he would be home before dark,
and set out.

The moors were autumn brown.
Only bits of green
showed here and there.
These were the pisky trails
and they stayed green as moss

the winter long.
Tom had heard about piskies.
They were the elves
who rode the moors at night
on their tiny ponies.

The lanterns they carried
as they galloped along
looked like fireflies.
"Dinky lights," people called them.
Tom had seen dinky lights
more than once,
but he had never seen a pisky.
And he hoped he never would.
The piskies led travelers astray.

Sometimes the travelers did not
get home until days later.
And sometimes they
did not get home at all.
No, Tom did not want
to meet up with a pisky.
He planned to leave the market
early and not ride late when
the piskies took over the moors.

Tom met many friends at the market.
They sat at the inn telling jokes
and stories and drinking cider.

Night came before he knew it.
It was pitch black
when Tom saddled Bess
and they started for the farm.
Bess was glad
to be going home.
Every now and then
she pricked up her ears
and whinnied.
"What is the matter, Bess?"
said Tom.
"Do you see something?"

Tom peered into the darkness.
At first he saw nothing.
Then, all at once,
dinky lights appeared.
The lights were moving swiftly.
They were coming closer and closer.

Tom reached over
and patted his mare.
"Don't worry, Bess," he said.
"I'll keep a strong hand
on the reins in case the piskies
want to try something."

Bess galloped on.
But in the middle of
the next moor, she whinnied
and arched her back.
Tom nearly fell off.
Suddenly he saw a pisky
on Bess's neck.
Then another and another.
One sat down between her ears.

They held dinky lanterns.
Small as the lanterns were,
they gave a strong light.

Tom saw the piskies clearly.
They were no larger
than the leprechaun.
They were brown-skinned
and whiskered. Their faces
and hands were wrinkled.
They wore green coats
and dark breeches.
And like the leprechauns,
they wore red peaked hats.

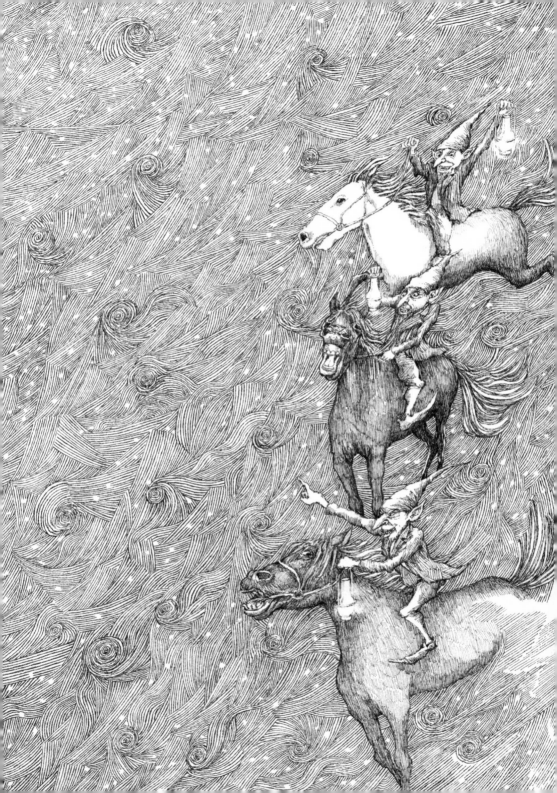

Tom held the reins firmly
and kept his eyes on the road.
Bess made strange sounds,
but she went bravely along.
Tom could hear the little men
talking and laughing.
Yet he could not make out
what they said.
He could see that the piskies
were tickling Bess.
But Bess kept to the path.

At last Tom heard his dog barking.
The dinky lanterns went out.
But Tom could still hear
pisky voices until they came
to the farmhouse gate.

When they reached the house,
Tom led Bess to the stable.
He lit the lantern.
The piskies were gone,
but Tom saw that Bess's mane
was braided into little tails.
Some of the tails
were looped into stirrups,
and some were woven
into tiny baskets.

That meant the piskies
had planned a long trip.
They had wanted to ride Bess,
and so they had tried
to make her throw Tom.

Tom patted Bess gratefully.
"You saved us from
the pisky mischief," he said.
He brushed her coat well
and combed out her mane.

"I promise we will not ride again
when the piskies are on the moors,"
Tom said.
He locked Bess safely in the stable
and took the key to bed with him.

Griselda was angry because
Tom came home so late.
"Piskies indeed!" she said,
when he told her
what had happened.
"That's cider talk.
I've never seen a pisky
and I've lived here all my life.
'Seeing is believing,' and
I don't believe in them."
"Well, I do!" said Tom.

And although Griselda refused
to believe in piskies,
she did not mind that Tom did.
For when Tom told her
the piskies were riding,
she knew
he would be staying home.
And she liked that.

ELIZABETH SHUB is a noted translator of folk and fairy tales. She adapted *Clever Kate* from the Brothers Grimm, and translated twelve of their tales in a collection entitled *About Wise Men and Simpletons*. Together with the author she has also translated many of the children's stories of Nobel prizewinner Isaac Bashevis Singer.

RACHEL ISADORA is the author/artist of several popular books for young children, including *Max*, an ALA Notable Book. Among her other picture books are *Ben's Trumpet* and *Backstage* by Robert Maiorano. Before becoming a full-time artist, Rachel Isadora was a professional ballerina.